MW00883861

Religion That's Real

A Study of the Book of James

MAURICE M. WHITE

WESTBOW
PRESS®
A DIVISION OF THOMAS NELSON
& ZONDERVAN

WestBow Press books may be ordered through booksellers or by contacting:

WestBow Press
A Division of Thomas Nelson & Zondervan
1663 Liberty Drive
Bloomington, IN 47403
www.westbowpress.com
1 (866) 928-1240

Scripture taken from the Holy Bible, New International Version®, NIV® Copyright© 1973, 1978, 1984, 2011 by Biblica, Inc.™ Used by permission of Zondervan. All rights reserved worldwide. WWW.ZONDERVAN.COM

Scriptures marked KJV are taken from the KING JAMES VERSION (KJV): KING JAMES VERSION, public domain.

ISBN: 978-1-5127-6168-9 (sc)
ISBN: 978-1-5127-6169-6 (hc)
ISBN: 978-1-5127-6167-2 (e)

Library of Congress Control Number: 2016917410

Print information available on the last page.

WestBow Press rev. date: 11/22/2016

FOREWORD

The awesome and always present Under-Girder of the universe, Revealer of himself to mankind, and the Sustainer of every life is the ultimate object of my gratitude for the honor to write this foreword. This book, "Religion That's Real", is authored by the Reverend Maurice White, whom I've known and observed since he was a preteen prodigy of a preacher. He surrendered his life early to Christ and has not wavered in that commitment.

Reverend White, served as a writer of Sunday School lessons for middle and high school students during my tenure as Managing Editor of NBCA Press, the publishing arm of National Baptist Convention of America. He was personally assigned to me by the late Dr. E. Edward Jones, Sr., the yet revered President of our convention for almost twenty years.

In this volume, "Religion That's Real", the reader is provided with both devotional inspirations and doctrinal insights as it relates to the treasured truths of God written in the epistle of James. The epistle of James is unique among all the books of the Bible, in that its writer held the dual distinction of being both a servant and a sibling of the Lord, Jesus Christ. The theme of the epistle of James is genuine faith, which is religion that's real.

This book consists of eleven enlightening, emancipating and empowering chapters. Five of the chapters I'm motivated to mention in particular.

Chapter one is titled "Count It All Joy". There the reader will find four practical principles that will provide the enablement to endure life's tensions in a world that's filled with troubles and terrors. There're constant conflicts in our culture and challenges in our lives, but you can still experience inward joy in the midst of it.

In chapter two, titled "The Origin of Temptation", the reader is reminded that temptations often begin with fascination, but always end with tragic devastation. Reverend White presents biblical testimony that "we are naughty by nature" and need the transforming power of God in our lives.

Chapter seven is titled "The Pink Tornado", which is the tongue. It has been said that it's the sticky and stinky subject that's in everybody's mouth. It's dangerous. It's divisive. It's destructive. In this book you'll learn biblical truth to keep it tamed.

Chapter nine is titled "When God is Defriended". The author states that the Bible speaks with crystal clarity that God wants to be our friend. He is the most faithful friend you'll ever find. Yet we live in a culture of social media where people delete friends daily. So, what happens when God is befriended? This is a chapter you'll read time and time again.

In the concluding chapter, titled "Real Faith", the author compares the unique examples of faith in Hebrews 11 with the undeniable evidences of faith presented by James. This book is an excellent thesis on "Religion That's Real".

October 2016
Dr. Prince A. Gipson, Jr.
Dean, Louisiana Baptist Ministers Leadership Conference
Founding Pastor, Christ Temple Missionary Baptist Church-Shreveport

INTRODUCTION

More now than ever the church is feeling the affects and effects of Postmodernism. No longer sitting in the pews are those who believe in absolutes such as right and wrong. No longer are our churches filled with people who believe in the authority of Scripture (the Bible). Postmodernism has caused the congregations of most main stream denominations to plateau and decline rapidly. Today, many people have what I like to call a Burger King mentality because they just want to have things their own way.

However, Postmodernism has also given people a desire for community and for what is real. People just simply want to be a part of something. Social media such as facebook, twitter, instagram, and snap chat are good indicators of people's desire for community. People are not seeking the complex and the complicated but they are hungry for the simple and practical. People want something real. Maybe that is why reality television shows are so popular. They also desire religion that is real.

James, the brother of Jesus, and author of the book of

James presents to us what real religion looks like. It is a religion that is not based upon rituals but a relationship with God. We are permitted to see a religion that does not glorify man but one that glorifies God. A religion that gives good news to the poor, sight to the spiritually blind, light to those who are in spiritual darkness, freedom to those in bondage, help for the helpless, and hope for the hopeless. It is a religion that is rooted and grounded in the life, ministry, and redemptive work of the Lord Jesus Christ.

CONTENTS

CHAPTER 1

Count It All Joy
James 1:1–12

One of the experiences that I cherish most from my childhood is attending Baptist Training Union. Every Sunday evening at five o'clock, saints both young and old would gather at the Shady Grove Baptist Church in Shreveport, Louisiana. It was a time for study, prayer, and singing the hymns of the church. I remember so clearly the raspy alto voice of Mrs. Effie Williams, the church pianist, singing triumphantly and joyfully:

This joy I have, the world didn't give it to me.
Oh, this joy I have, the world didn't give it to me.
Since the world didn't give it,
The world can't take it away!

This is the same type of joy that James urges and challenges Christians to have in difficult times. James says, "Consider it pure joy, my brothers and sisters, whenever you face trials of many kinds" (James 1:2 NIV). This is a call for us to defy the norm when facing multifaceted and multicolored trials. Sorrow, sadness, or sulking is the norm, but James encourages us to have joy as we take inventory of our infirmities, calculate our crisis, and tabulate our troubles. In James 1:2–12, the apostle and pillar of the early church offers four things Christians must do in order to count it all joy!

We Must Know Some Things

No matter how old and antiquated we are, all of us have a little kid in us. Even now, well past the age of thirty, I find myself attentively and happily watching cartoons with the kids. On any given day, most of the televisions in my home are on Disney or Nick Jr. I recall as a child getting up very early on Saturday mornings—before the sun had peaked the eastern sky, and while the birds were chirping—to watch my favorite cartoon, *G.I. Joe*. There were some intense battles waged between the Joes and Cobra, but what I remember most is a quote from the cartoon that says, "Now you know, and knowing is half the battle." Oh, what an awesome day it will be when Christians embrace that knowing there is a purpose and reason for what we go through in life gives us an advantage on life's battlefield. What is the purpose for manifold, multifaceted, multicolored trials? James says, "Because you know that the testing of your faith produces perseverance" (James 1:3 NIV).

The Greek reveals to us that James uses the active voice when he says in the text "knowing." The active voice means that the subject is the doer of the action. Therefore, *knowing* is something we must do for ourselves. It is a lesson that can't be learned from a book or in a classroom. The experiences and vicissitudes of life test our faith and eventually produce patience. God tests our faith as He also tested the faith of the Jewish patriarch Abraham when God commanded Abraham to offer the promised son Isaac as a sacrifice on Mount Moriah. Yet Abraham trusted God, because he knew something. Hebrews 11:17–19 (NIV) says, "By faith Abraham, when God tested him, offered Isaac as a sacrifice. He who had embraced the promises was about to sacrifice his one and only son, even though God had said to him, 'It is through Isaac that your offspring will be reckoned.' Abraham reasoned that God could even raise the dead, and so in manner of speaking he did receive Isaac back from the dead." Abraham passed the test, but what about you and me?

The test is meant to make us better, not worse; stronger, not weaker; wise, not foolish; faithful, not faithless; patient, not impatient; and mature, not immature. Don't come out of the purifying fire the same way you went in! Don't come out with the same hangups, insecurities, doubts, and shortcomings! James's desire is for us to come out complete, lacking nothing, and mature. If you want to see an immature Christian, then look at a Christian who is plagued by impatience, anxiety, and worry.

The teachings and theology of Paul and Peter line up with that of James, because both knew some things. Paul says in Romans 5:3–4 (NIV), "Not only so, but we glory in our sufferings, because we know that suffering produces perseverance, character; and character, hope." When the seeds of suffering are planted in our lives, the hope of the fruit that will be produced makes the season of suffering a little easier to bear. Peter knew that our times of testing prove the authenticity of our faith. "In all this you greatly rejoice, though now for a little while you may have had to suffer grief in all kinds of trials. These have come so that the proven genuineness of your faith of greater worth than gold, which perishes even though refined by fire may result in praise, glory and honor when Jesus Christ is revealed" (1 Peter 1:6–7 NIV). It's easy to have faith when the grass is green, the flowers are tall, and the sun's rays shine brightly in your life. But can you trust God when the grass has withered, the tall flowers have fallen, and the rays of the sun have been eclipsed by rolling dark clouds?

We Must Have Unwavering Faith

Faith is something that every believer in Christ needs. We need faith because faith gives us hope. We need faith, because faith gives us a good, real, and relevant testimony. We need faith to understand and accept that the world did not come into being by way of evolution, a big bang, or the procession of the equinoxes; rather, it was God's

4

omnipotent, divine speech that ushered the universe into existence. We need faith, because without faith, it is impossible to please God. However, sadly and unfortunately, we don't possess the type of faith to count it all joy and to get God's attention in prayer. Faith is the great attention-getter in the prayer life of the believer. James makes the argument that not just any type of faith gets the attention of God, but it is unwavering faith that gets the Master's undivided attention.

James's in-depth knowledge of the Hebrew scriptures and the rich Jewish heritage rises to the surface as he declares, "If any of you lacks wisdom, you should ask God" (James 1:5 NIV). Surely, James must have had in mind that dark, cold night in Gibeon, in 1 Kings 3, when King Solomon did not ask God for long life, riches, or the lives of his enemies but instead for wisdom. God did indeed grant Solomon's request for wisdom. First Kings 10:24 (NIV) says, "The whole world sought audience with Solomon to hear the wisdom God had put in his heart." Heavenly wisdom from above—not wisdom from below or of the world—is a necessity if we are going to count all joy. Rejoice! Praise God! Shout hallelujah! God not only gives wisdom when we ask. Whatever we ask for in faith, according to His will, He will grant. James adheres to his big brother's advice: "Ask and it will be given to you; seek and you will find; knock and the door will be opened to you" (Matthew 7:7 NIV).

Notice if you will that we must ask in faith, nothing

wavering. Have you ever wondered why your prayers were not being answered? First, unanswered prayer is a result of praying outside of the will of God. "When you ask, you do not receive, because you ask with wrong motives, that you may spend what you get on your pleasures" (James 4:3). The same lust that leads us to sin and death also leads us to unanswered prayer. Ask yourself this question: *what sin in my life is preventing my prayer from being answered by God?* Second, unanswered prayer is caused by wavering faith. This type of faith is that of an unstable or double-minded person—a Christian who has a bipolar spiritual life. And the only prescription for this type of spiritual life is faith. James wants us to know that the person who thinks that he or she has faith and fear, trust and doubt, contentment and anxiety, and love for God and for the world simultaneously will not receive anything from the Lord. So the next time you pray, don't spend time arguing, disputing, complaining, and talking to yourself. But as that great hymn of the church says, "Have a little talk with Jesus!"

I may have doubts and fears, my eyes be filled with tears,
But Jesus is a friend who watches day and night.
I go to Him in prayer; He knows my every care.
And just a little talk with my Jesus makes it right.
Have a little talk with Jesus …
Find a little talk with Jesus makes it right.

We Must Rejoice in Spite of Our Socioeconomic Background

James not only reveals that we face multifaceted, multicolored, and manifold trials, but also that the body of Christ is made up of people from all walks of life. Educated and uneducated, black and white, short and tall, big and small, rich and poor can make up an assembly or body of believers. The portrait that James paints is of a poor Christian and rich Christian rejoicing in the Lord. The Christian from a low socioeconomic background is able to boast in the Lord, because he or she has been exalted. Our position in Christ far outweighs our position in poverty or status in society. Who we are in Christ allows us to transcend even the most impoverished situations. Why? Although we may not have the biggest bank account, car, or house, Paul speaks of the poor individual's exaltation as God taking us from rags to riches spiritually. The great apostle and missionary of the early church says in the opening of his letter to the church at Ephesus, "Praise be to the God and Father of our Lord Jesus Christ, who has blessed us in the heavenly realms with every spiritual blessing in Christ" (Ephesians 1:3 NIV).

The recipients of James's letter were probably shocked and thought it somewhat strange to hear of a rich Christian rejoicing. Wealth and high social status were not common among Christians in the first century. However, James shines a light on the rich brother who rejoices or boasts not because of his material possession, but because he is made low. He rejoices over the opportunity to be humiliated for the sake of the gospel of Christ. Knowing that riches will wither as the grass and fall as the flower, but suffering for Christ brings eternal reward. "For I reckon that the sufferings of this present time are not worthy to be compared with the glory which shall be revealed in us" (Romans 8:18). In the beatitudes of Jesus's most famous sermon, entitled "The Sermon on the Mount," the Master Teacher educates us: "Blessed are you when people insult you, persecute you and falsely say all kinds of evil against you because of me. Rejoice and be glad, because great is your reward in heaven, for in the same way they persecuted the prophets who were before you" (Matthew 5:11–12 NIV).

We Must Endure Trials

James gives a blessing in his writing for both rich and poor Christians who rejoice in Christ. "Blessed is the one who perseveres under trial because, having stood the test, that person will receive the crown of life that the Lord has promised to those who love him" (James 1:12 NIV). In many instances, James's writing is oxymoronic in nature. He often speaks of things that just don't seem to go together. He talks about joy and trials in James 1:2. Now he mentions blessings and trials. What's up with all these oxymorons? Could it be that the goal of James is to reshape how we view trials? He wants us to view trials not in a negative light but in a positive one. Only with

God's help can we transform trials, tribulation, adversity, and affliction into something positive. God helps us by providing encouragement so we will not be sorrowful but joyful. "Consider it pure joy" (James 1:2 NIV). God helps us by providing enlightenment so we will understand life's trials. "If any of you lacks wisdom, you should ask God" (James 1:5 NIV). God helps us by providing energy for us to endure trials. "Blessed is the one that perseveres" (James 1:12 NIV).

The word *endure* used by James is the Greek word *hupomeno,* a compound word; *hupo* means "under," and *meno* means "to remain." The blessing is not leaving or being delivered from the trial but remaining under the weight of adversity and affliction. How do we endure when the weight of the world is upon our shoulders? The key is to be fearless, forbearing, and faithful.

When we are fearless, we face difficulties, danger, distress, and despair head-on. King David's fearlessness was rooted and grounded in his relationship with the self existing and eternal God of Israel. David poetically expresses his fearlessness in Psalm 27:1 (KJV): "The LORD is my light and my salvation; whom shall I fear? The LORD is the strength of my life; of whom shall I be afraid? I can endure when God is my direction in darkness, deliverance from danger, and defense against the devil.

When we are forbearing, we patiently wait on God. David says, "I waited patiently for the LORD; and he inclined unto me, and heard my cry" (Psalm 40:1 KJV).

David paints for us a very clear, concise, beautiful portrait of God bending over His people as we wait for Him to deliver us from trials. God does not bend to hear us better but to show us that He cares. When you know that God cares, the burdens of life are not so heavy to bear. "Casting all your care upon him; for he careth for you" (1 Peter 5:7 KJV). Psalm 55:2 (KJV) assures us, "Cast thy burden upon the LORD, and he shall sustain thee: he shall never suffer the righteous to be moved.

When we are faithful, we endure without allowing trials to affect or threaten our commitment to God. How do we know when trials negatively affect our relationship with God? First, we start tipping God instead of tithing to God. Next, we know that enduring trials has a negative impact when we start seeking relief through inappropriate actions and relationships. We are headed down the wrong road when we start worshipping the creation instead of the Creator. When Sunday morning worship and Wednesday night prayer meeting and Bible study are placed on the back burner, we are most definitely in trouble.

For the past week and a half, the Summer Olympic Games have been going on in London, England. I have had the opportunity to sit down watch some of the best athletes in the world perform on the world's greatest and largest athletic stage. It's been great watching Gabby Douglas, Serena Williams, and others win gold for the US, even in spite of NBC's dreaded taped delay. The most exciting event to watch was American swimmer Michael

Phelps swimming in the last Olympic individual event of his career. It was the hundred-meter butterfly, and when Michael Phelps made the turn at the wall with fifty meters to go in the race, he was in seventh place, on his way to an embarrassing end to an awesome career in swimming. But Michael Phelps didn't give up or give in; he just continued to swim. Phelps was in seventh place at the turn, but he finished the race first, winning his twenty-first medal and seventeenth gold. Why? Because he endured to the end.

God has a reward, a crown of life, waiting for those of us who endure the trials of this life. Trials are inevitable, so count it all joy. It comes with the territory of being a Christian. They are inseparable from discipleship, because Jesus says, "If any man will come after me, let him deny himself, and take up his cross, and follow me" (Matthew 17:24 KJV).

CHAPTER 2

The Origin of Temptation
James 1:13–15

Ancient Greek mythology introduces to us a half-woman, half0bird mystical creature called the siren. The sirens were known for their ability to produce a sweet song that lured many Greek mariners to their deaths. It is believed that when passing ships came near the island of the sirens, the sweet sound produced by these creatures caused ships to change their courses, which inevitably and tragically led to the destruction of the ships on the rocks surrounding the island. The Greek hero Odysseus wanted to hear the sweet sound of the sirens so badly that he ordered his men to put wax in their ears and tie him to the mast of the ship in order to stay on course so he could hear the sirens as they passed the island.

The temptation that lures believers off course can often seem to be very sweet; yet the reality is that it really leads to destruction. Religion that is genuine and true can appear to be fake and phony when we give in to temptation. Such

13

a lifestyle causes sinners to question our Christianity. *I thought they were supposed to be Christians. Don't they attend Zion Traveler Baptist Church on Sundays? Then why are they acting this way?* Or in the words of Gandhi, "Christians are the most un-Christlike people in the world." So our religion can be real, we must discover the source of temptation. Knowing the source of temptation will help us to resist it when it comes.

> Yield not to temptation, for yielding is sin;
> Each vict'ry will help you some other to win.
> Fight manfully onward, dark passions subdue;
> Look ever to Jesus, He will carry you through.
> Ask the Savior to help you,
> Comfort, strengthen, and keep you;
> He is willing to aid you.
> He will carry you through.

Where Temptation Does Not Come From

James begins by refuting a heresy being taught among the twelve tribes scattered abroad. Apparently, there were some Christians in the first century trying to blame God for their temptation and sin. They engaged in this type of thing because many felt that the trials sent into their lives by God caused their sin. Even in the midst of trials, God who is sovereign gives us the right to choose. As free will moral agents, we have the right to choose between good or bad, right or wrong, godliness or ungodliness, righteousness or unrighteousness. In the most assertive way possible, James says, "Let no man say when his tempted, I am tempted of God." Temptation does not come from God.

The book of James is a very practical book with real life lessons to be learned by every believer. However, the epistle is also filled with a plethora of theology. When we consider the character and nature of God, we can come to only one conclusion concerning temptation: He is not the source.

God is *eternal*. "LORD, thou hast been our dwelling place in all generations. Before the mountains were brought forth, or ever thou hadst formed the earth and the world, even from everlasting to everlasting, thou art God" (Psalm 90:1–2 KJV).

God is *immutable* (changeless). "For I am the LORD, I change not; therefore ye sons of Jacob are not consumed" (Malachi 3:6 KJV).

God is *omniscient* (all-knowing). "O LORD, thou hast searched me, and known me. Thou knowest my downsitting and mine uprising, thou understandest my thought afar off. Thou compassest my path and my lying down, and art acquainted with all my ways. For there is not a word in my tongue, but, lo, O LORD, thou knowest it altogether. Thou hast beset me behind and before, and laid thine hand upon me. Such knowledge is too wonderful for me; it is high, I cannot attain unto it" (Psalm 139:1–6 KJV).

God is *omnipresent* (everywhere). "Whither shall I go from thy spirit? or whither shall I flee from thy presence? If

I ascend up into heaven, thou art there: if I make my bed in hell, behold, thou art there. If I take the wings of the morning, and dwell in the uttermost parts of the sea; Even there shall thy hand lead me, and thy right hand shall hold me" (Psalm 139:7–10 KJV).

God is *omnipotent* (all-powerful). "Is any thing too hard for the LORD? At the time appointed I will return unto thee, according to the time of life, and Sarah shall have a son" (Genesis 18:14 KJV).

God is *holy*. The attribute of God that defends James' argument in the text is the undeniable, unquestionable, uncontestable fact that God is holy. "For God cannot be tempted with evil, neither tempteth he any man"—because He is holy. All throughout the inspired words of scripture, the holiness of God is proclaimed. After God's mighty hand opened up the Red Sea and brought the Hebrews out of Egyptian bondage, Moses, in a song of praise, speaks of the holiness of God. "Who among the gods is like you, LORD? Who is like you majestic in holiness, awesome in glory, working wonders?" (Exodus 15:11 NIV) Emphatically and unashamedly, there is only one response to these two questions: there is nobody or no one like God. None of the idolatrous gods of this world can be compared to our God. Hear the prophetic voice of Isaiah: "With whom then, will you compare God? To what image will you liken him" (Isaiah 40:18 NIV). Hallelujah! God cannot be matched in power, knowledge, grace, mercy, or holiness. God is unique in holiness, unmatched in righteousness, and unyielding and upright in justice. If God is holy, then we must conclude that temptation does not come from Him, because sin and evil are the antithesis of His divine and holy nature.

God *hates sin*. Simply put, temptation does not come from God, because He hates sin. Notice if you will that God does not hate the sinner but sin. Consider this proverbial saying: "There are six things the LORD hates, seven that are detestable to him: haughty eyes, a lying tongue, hands that shed innocent blood, a heart that devises wicked schemes, feet that are quick to rush into evil, a false witness who pours out lies and a person who stirs up conflict in the community" (Proverbs 6:16–19 NIV). Sin disgusts, irritates, agitates, and annoys the Holy One of Israel. And the challenge put forth to we who are God's people is this: "You shall be holy, for I the LORD your God am Holy."

When we speak of being holy or holiness within the context of the New Testament, it does us good to examine what Bible scholars and theologians call the doctrine of sanctification. What does sanctification mean? It means to be sacred, consecrated, or even separated from something. Through sanctification, God saves or separates us from sin. God has saved us from the penalty of sin, is saving us from the power of sin, and will save us from the presence of sin! The goal of sanctification is best stated by Paul in Philippians 1:6 (NIV): "Being confident of this, that he who began a good work in you will carry it on to completion until the day of Christ Jesus." When we think about it logically, why would God, who delivers us from sin, tempt us to sin? Saints of God, it does not make sense.

Where Temptation Begins

If our religion is going to be real, then we must stop playing the blame game. Stop blaming God and everyone else for your mistakes, failures, and sins. We have nobody to blame but ourselves. What a tough pill to swallow in a culture where people do not want to take responsibility for their actions.

James reveals to us that the source of temptation is not external but internal. "But each person is tempted when they are dragged away by their own evil desire and enticed" (James 1:14 NIV). We are not tempted by the evil desires of our friend or neighbors but by our own desires. Temptation begins with our own sin nature. Wow! What a shocking revelation! The Devil did not make me do it!

Whether we want to admit it or not, whether we want to accept or reject it, we are naughty by nature. We are born into this world with a nature and desires that are in direct contrast to the nature and character of God. In his moment of confession and contrition, King David says, "Surely I was sinful at birth, sinful from the time my mother conceived me" (Psalm 51:5 NIV). In his letter to the Christians living in Rome, Paul admits there is a constant and daily struggle within us between the old nature (the flesh) and the new nature (the Holy Spirit). "For in my inner being I delight in God's law; but I see another law at work in me, waging war against the law of my mind and making me a prisoner of the law of sin at work within me"(Romans 7:22–23 NIV). The sad reality is that by nature, we are born murderers, adulterers, liars, whoremongers, gossipers, fornicators, and homosexuals.

On Monday nights at six o'clock at Zion Traveler Baptist Church in Ruston, Louisiana, where the Lord has allowed me to serve as pastor for the past nine years, we have a recreation ministry for boys called Bible and Basketball. Some of the men of our church get together with the boys to study the Bible and play basketball. One of the young boys was puzzled by something that was said by one of his female classmates at school. The girl claimed to have been born a lesbian. One of the men leading the discussion, being guided by the Holy Spirit, responded quickly, "If she was born a lesbian, then it is good to know that she can be born again by the power of the Holy Spirit."

Nicodemus, on the night when he met Jesus in some secluded, dark place in Jerusalem, was informed of the same fact. Jesus told Nicodemous, "Very truly I tell you, no one can enter the kingdom of God unless they are born of water and the Spirit. Flesh gives birth to flesh, but the Spirit gives birth to spirit. You should not be surprised at my saying, 'You must be born again!'" (John 3:5–7 NIV)

If the old, sinful nature is not held in check by the new nature, then it will be very easy for us to be dragged away or baited by temptation. Just as hunters use corn to bait deer and fishermen us worms to catch fish, the Devil knows what to use in order to entice us to sin. Consider the words of John the beloved in 1 John 2:16 (NIV): "For everything in the world-the lust of the flesh, the lust of the eyes, and the pride of life-comes not from the Father but from the world." "The lust of the flesh" means we are enticed by sinful appetites. "The lust of the eyes" means we are enticed by sinful attractions. "The pride of life" means we are enticed by sinful ambitions.

Real religion is personified in the life and ministry of Jesus, who has given us an example to be followed. When Satan tempted the Lord in the wilderness, Jesus's response to the temptation on every occasion was, "It is written." The inspired Word of God is our only defense against temptation. Therefore, we must read, study, memorize, meditate on, apply, and live the Word.

Where Temptation Leads Us

James begins James 1:15 with the adverb "then" to usher in a succession of events that will transpire once temptation has gotten the best of us. The logical yet deadly succession is as follows: temptation leads to sin, and sin leads to death, a road that is difficult to get off of once the journey begins.

What does James mean when he says, "Then, after desire has conceived, it gives birth to sin; and sin, when it is full-grown, gives birth to death" (James 1:15 NIV)?

Legally, James suggests that temptation gets the best

of us when we are arrested, enslaved, or literally captured by our sinful appetites, attractions, and ambitions. The word "conceived" used here by James is the Greek word *sullambano*, which literally means "to clasp, seize, arrest, or capture." Once temptation gets the handcuffs on us, it is extremely hard to get them off.

Biologically, when temptation captures us, the conception of sin becomes an inevitable reality. It is the idea of a mother bringing forth a child from her womb. Agriculturally, it also conveys the picture of the earth bringing forth fruit. Wherever the seed of temptation is planted, nourished, watered, and cultivated, the result will always be sin.

I must warn you that there is a big difference between bearing children or plants and to bear sin. There is much travail and pain involved when bearing children, but the end result is joy. The farmer who spends countless hours and numerous resources planting and watering knows it was well worth it when the harvest comes. However, this is not the case with giving in to temptation. Giving in to temptation may seem fun, exciting, easy, and even pleasurable at the time, but the end result is never joy but sorrow. Listen to the tragic words of James, "and sin, when it is finished ..." When sin is finished, marriages are messed up. When sin is finished, reputations are ruined. When sin is finished, testimonies are tainted. When sin is finished, lives are lost.

James does well to warn us not to err, because the

ultimate result of sin is physical, spiritual, and eternal death. My childhood pastor often reminded us, "Sin will make you stay longer than you intended to stay and pay more than you intended to pay." Real religion chooses to live and not die.

CHAPTER 3

The God Who Keeps on Giving
James 1:16–18

Down through the years, Christians have used clothes, jewelry, license plates, and many other means to express and share our faith in Jesus with the world. Today, it has become popular for young believers to wear bracelets with symbols on them displaying in a nutshell the redemptive work of Jesus Christ. I'm pretty sure you have seen these images before. The arrow pointing down represents Christ coming into the world by way of the virgin birth. Next, there is a cross that reminds us of Christ's sacrificial and vicarious death. And of course, there is the image of the empty tomb, which symbolizes His resurrection from the dead. The arrow pointing up represents the ascension of the Lord, and the second arrow looks forward with great expectation and anticipation to the second coming of the Lord Jesus.

During my time as a young believer and teenager, we also wore bracelets to express our faith. The bracelets simply had the letters *WWJD* written on them. What would Jesus do? It was a reminder to us that whatever, whenever, or wherever we encountered a challenging situation in life, we should ask ourselves the question, "What would Jesus do?" Living, serving, praying, loving, forgiving, and giving like Jesus are good ways for our religion to be real and relevant.

The world would be a different place if we were givers like God! One of the most awesome gifts that God has given to us is life. The same physical, spiritual, and eternal life that sin desires to rob us of, God gives to us lovingly and freely. God gives us physical life. Job 33:4 (NIV) says, "The Spirit of God has made me; the breath of the Almighty gives me life." God gifts us with spiritual life. Ephesians 2:1 (NIV) says, "As for you, you were dead in your transgressions and sins." Finally, God grants us eternal life. John 3:16 (NIV) says, "For God so loved the world that he gave his one and only Son, that whoever believes in him shall not perish but have eternal life."

Not only is God the giver of life, but also the giver of wisdom. According to James, wisdom is a gift from God. It is a gift that God gives to us generously and liberally if we ask Him. "If any of you lacks wisdom, you should ask God, who gives generously to all without finding fault, and it will be given you" (James 1:5 NIV).

Gifts such as life and wisdom, unlike temptation, do not originate inside of us but above us. The gifts are heavenly! Therefore, we must know the nature of the gift, the Giver, and the receiver to fully understand why God keeps on giving.

The Nature of the Gift

"Set your minds on things above, not on earthly things" (Colossians 3:2 NIV). These are the words of the apostle Paul to the church at Colossae as he challenges Christians to have mindsets that are not worldly but heavenly. Children of God, we would do well to listen to the words of Paul, because the truth of the matter is that this world is not our home. We are only pilgrims traveling through this world on our way to the world to come. Therefore, the desire of the Christian's religion that is real must be heaven.

Real religion desires heavenly treasure. Matthew 6:20– 21 (NIV) says, "But store up for yourselves in heaven, where moths and vermin do not destroy, and where thieves do not break in and steal. For where your treasure is, there your heart will be also." Real religion also desires heavenly blessings. Ephesians 1:3 (NIV) says, "Praise be to the God and Father of our Lord Jesus Christ, who has blessed us in the heavenly realms with every spiritual blessing in Christ."

Real religion desires heavenly wisdom. James 3:17 (NIV) says, "But the wisdom that comes from heaven first of all pure; then peace-loving, considerate, submissive, full of mercy and good fruit, impartial and sincere." Finally, real religion desires heavenly gifts. James 1:17 (NIV) says, "Every good and perfect gift is from above."

James describes the nature of the gift that God gives to us from above as good and perfect gifts. Whenever and whatever God gives is always good, because by nature, God is good. Millard Erickson, in his systematic theology, suggests that God's goodness is based upon His moral purity, which means that God is absolutely free from anything wicked or evil. Erickson also states that the goodness of God is based upon His absolute purity. According to Erickson, "This means that he is untouched and unstained by the evil in the world." Therefore, we must conclude that whatever God does is good. Since the beginning of time, good has been what God sends into the lives of His people. Some seven times in the creation narrative of Genesis 1, Moses says, "And God saw it was good." God is worthy of all praise, because He continues to do good, and we should never forget the goodness of God. Grace, mercy, love, salvation, faith, and hope are all good gifts that God sends into our lives. And know this one thing, saints of God—even when bad things happen in our lives, when God is in the mix, "all things work together for good" (Romans 8:28 NIV).

God's gifts, according to James, are also perfect. By using this word, James wants us to understand that the gifts from above are complete and not lacking in any form or fashion. As a matter of fact, when we trace the Greek word used for "perfect," it shows us that the gifts God blesses us with are given for a reason. We should always be aware of the fact that there is a divine purpose and plan behind the gifts God gives. The gifts are a means that God uses to bring His plan for our lives into fruition. What is the divine purpose? The purpose is to bring us to full maturity in Jesus Christ.

The Nature of the Giver

Only a good and perfect God can give good and perfect gifts. James identifies God as "the Father of lights." What a fitting name for God, who is the giver of both life and light. John expresses this theological truth in John 1:4 (NIV): "In Him was life and the life was the light of all mankind." Through Jesus Christ, the incarnate Son of God, God the Father brought light into a spiritually dark world. "The light shines in the darkness, and the darkness has not overcome it" (John 1:5 NIV). Hallelujah! Jesus is the light of the world!

One of the heavenly gifts that God bestows upon us is the blessed honor and privilege of letting His light shine through us when our religion is real. "In the same way, let your light shine before others, that they may see your good deeds and glorify your Father in heaven" (Matthew 5:16 NIV). When our religion is real, through good works, people are able to see and experience the glory of God. And it is safe to conclude that those who truly experience the glory of God will take notice of the immutability of God. They will clearly see that God does not change.

The book of James is practical, but it is also very

theological. From a theological perspective, James deals with the issue of knowing what God is like. What is God like? In James 1:13, when James reveals to us that neither temptation nor sin originates with God, he teaches us about the holiness of God. In James 1:17, he teaches us that God is immutable. God does not change! "Every good and perfect gift is from above, coming down from the Father of the heavenly lights, who does not change like shifting shadows" (James 1:17 NIV). God is not fickle. There is no evolution or revolution with God. Malachi 3:6 (NIV) says, "I the LORD do not change. So you, the descendants of Jacob, are not destroyed." Hebrew 13:8 (NIV) says, "Jesus Christ is the same yesterday and today and forever."

Real religion can be reality in our lives when we accept the faithful fact that Jesus Christ is the God of yesterday, today, and tomorrow. Why is it so hard for people to accept the immutability of God in these times in which we live? It is difficult because we live in a culture that changes rapidly. Times and things evolve so quickly that we wrongly believe that what was good yesterday is no longer good today. Consider the following examples of how things change constantly.

- How we listen to our music has changed greatly. Our parents listened to records and eight-tracks. Growing up in the '90s, we listened to tapes and CDs. Now our favorite songs can be simply downloaded on our electronic devices.

- People seem to upgrade their cell phones constantly. The latest Android, Galaxy, or iPhone is almost obsolete before it has even been in stores for a few months.
- The world is no longer analog; everything has now gone digital.

Cell phones, tablets, and televisions may have to be upgraded, but we can rejoice because we will never have to upgrade or change our God. The same truth, grace, mercy, and love that God provided for us yesterday is good today and will be good tomorrow.

The Nature of the Receiver

We serve an immutable God who has power to cause change in fickle and wavering people. How does God cause change in those who are the recipients of His good and perfect gifts? God changes us through new birth. It is by way of new birth that God imparts unto us a new nature. God, of His own will and volition, chooses to give us new life through Jesus Christ. In essence, we become new creatures. James declares, "He chose to give us birth through the word of truth, that we might be a kind of first fruits of all he created" (James 1:18 NIV).

The Holy Spirit, a gift that God has given to all believers, plays a significant role in our regeneration or being made new. Paul says to his son in the ministry, Titus, who was the pastor of the church in Crete, "He saved us, not because of righteous things we have done, but because of mercy. He saved us through the washing of rebirth and renewal by the Holy Spirit." God does not upgrade, fix, or modify us but makes us brand-new. "Therefore, if anyone is in Christ, the new creation has come. The old has gone, the new is here!" (2 Corinthians 5:17 NIV) The new is here! Hallelujah! Our religion can be real, because God has given us a new walk, talk, mind, heart, way of doing things, ambitions, and goals.

The seed of sin produces death, but the seed of God's Word brings new life. Therefore, we have the great privilege and responsibility of sharing the gift of God's unchanging and life-giving Word with a dark and spiritually dead world. If our religion is real, the best gift we could ever give to anyone is God's eternal, universal, and historical truth, for the truth of God's Word has made all the difference in our lives. "And you also were included in Christ when you heard the message of truth, the gospel of your salvation" (Ephesians 1:13 NIV).

CHAPTER 4

Fighting Your Worst Enemy
James 1:19–27

A few days ago, I found myself flipping through the channels, trying to find something to watch on television. Being the sports fanatic that I am, I stumbled upon an interview of some football coaches from the SEC, which is the Southeastern Athletic Conference. The commentator hosting the show asked the coaches, "What is the hardest thing about coaching very talented student athletes?"

One of the coaches responded, "The hardest thing is getting a talented guy to see that he is his own worst enemy. He is the only one keeping him from reaching his full potential."

I believe that is not only the case in the game of college football, but also the game of life. In spite of how gifted or talented we may be, our worst enemies can often be ourselves. This is a crucial point that James attempts to drive home earlier in this book when he speaks of us being dragged away by our own lusts. In the same way,

31

self-righteousness and self-centeredness stand in the way of our religion being real.

Self-righteousness will be one of the main reasons many will lift up their eyes in hell. Tragically, there are people today who believe that they can make it on their own. They feel as if they don't need Jesus! Oh, how wrong they are!

In Luke 12, Jesus tells a parable about a very self-centered rich man. How do we know that the man was self-centered? He never mentions anyone else but only speaks of "I" and "my." "What shall I do?" "This is what I'll do." "I will tear down my barns and build bigger ones." "I will store." "And I will say to myself …"

On that night, he learns the tragic end of his self-centeredness. Jesus says, on that night, God said to him, "You fool! This very night, your life will be demanded from you. Then you will get what you have prepared for yourself." Jesus informs us that this is the tragic end of those who focus on self and not on God.

Being a disciple and follower of Christ also requires us to deal with self. One of the requirements of discipleship given by Jesus is that a man must deny himself. Listen to this hard saying of Jesus: "Whoever wants to be my disciple must deny themselves and take up their cross daily and follow me" (Luke 9:23 NIV). The Greek word *aparneomai* used here by Jesus is the same word used by Him on the eve of the crucifixion when He foretold of Peter's denial. The same intensity and passion used by Peter when he denied Jesus three times should be used by us to disown and abstain from ourselves.

I love the way John the Baptist puts in John 3:30, "He must become greater; I must become less" (NIV). The greater Jesus becomes in our lives, the more real our religion will be.

When Jesus becomes greater, then it becomes easier to win the victory over self-righteousness and self-centeredness. I believe James shows us how to measure whether we are being led by the flesh (self) or the Spirit. Jesus becomes greater, and we become less when there is self-control, self-evaluation, and self-sacrifice in our lives.

Self-Control

Allowing the Holy Spirit to control our emotions is key to us impacting the world with the gospel of Jesus Christ. Unstable and weak faith ultimately leads to emotions that are all over the place. However, stable and strong faith manifests itself in a person who is, as James says, "quick to listen, slow to speak and slow to be angry" (James 1:19 NIV).

Listening is so important because "Consequently, faith comes from hearing the message, and the message is heard through the word about Christ" (Romans 10:17 NIV). Later on in this chapter, James challenges us to be more than hearers but to be doers of the Word of God. So the question we must ask ourselves is this: how do we know when our faith has been strengthened by listening to the Word of God? We know when listening becomes more of a priority than speaking and becoming angry. Simply put, we cannot allow wrath or anger to rule and reign in our lives.

Religion that is real exhibits great self-control because of the negative impact that anger can have on our personal testimonies. As a matter of fact, all throughout the Bible, we are warned about anger, especially in the wisdom given to us by way of the book of Proverbs.

Anger Acts Foolishly

Proverbs 14:16–17 (NIV) says, "The wise fear the LORD and shun evil, but a fool is hotheaded and yet feels secure. A quick-tempered person does foolish things, and the one who devises evil schemes is hated." Proverbs 14:29 (NIV) adds, "Whoever is patient has great understanding, but one who is quick-tempered displays folly."

Anger Creates Friction

Proverbs 29:22 (NIV) states, "An angry person stirs up conflict, and a hot-tempered person commits many sins." And Proverbs 30:33 (NIV) tells us, "For as churning cream produces butter, and as twisting the nose produces blood, so stirring up anger produces strife."

Wise people will not let anger get the best of them, because they understand that the world is watching to see what type of fruit we have on our trees. Real religion produces the righteousness of God. It is the type of righteous that was revealed to the world through Jesus Christ. "For in the gospel the righteousness of God is revealed a

RELIGION THAT'S REAL

righteousness that is by faith from first to last, "just as it is written: "The righteous live by faith" (Romans 1:17 NIV). James lets us know that anger does not produce this type of righteousness, "because human anger does not produce the righteousness that God desires" (James 1:20 NIV).

Deductive reasoning teaches us that if anger does not produce righteousness, then it must produce unrighteousness. And we are commanded by James to literally take off or do away with unrighteousness. Dirtiness and depravity in the life of the believer who has real religion must be things of the past. Moral filth and evil must be replaced by the Word of God. The inspired Word of God implanted in our hearts and minds is able to save, heal, protect, preserve, and deliver us!

Self-Evaluation

The late pop singer Michael Jackson had a very popular song entitled "Man in the Mirror." The lyrics to that song are powerful: "I'm starting with the man in the mirror; I'm asking him to change his ways … If you wanna make the world a better place, take a look at yourself, and then make a change." Real religion most definitely starts with the person in the mirror.

James urges the saints of the first century to change. The passionate plea is for them to not be just hearers of the Word, but also doers. It is a call for believers to take a look at ourselves in the mirror. Too often, we neglect

35

James's purposeful practice of self-evaluation because we would rather look into a microscope and not in a mirror. We aggressively and wrongly evaluate and judge the lives of others, a practice that is contrary to the teachings of Jesus and Paul. In the Sermon on the Mount, Jesus commands, "Do not judge, or you too will be judged. For in the same way you judge others, you will be judged, and with the measure you use, it will be measured to you" (Matthew 7:1–2 NIV). Paul echoes the divine teaching of Christ when he warns, "You, therefore, have no excuse, you who pass judgment on someone else, you are condemning yourself, because you who pass judgment do the same things" (Romans 2:1 NIV). Self-evaluation never occurs when we look into microscopes.

Self-evaluation is also evaded when we spend too much time looking into the rearview mirror. Too much time spent focusing on the past prevents us from tackling the problems of the present or moving forward to a future filled with purpose. In Philippians 3, Paul gives us some good advice concerning not being crippled by the past. He speaks of a continuing journey and perpetual quest to know Christ. "Brothers and sisters, I do not consider myself yet to have taken hold of it. But one thing I do: Forgetting what is behind and straining toward what is ahead, I press toward the goal to win the prize for which God has called me heavenward in Christ Jesus" (Philippians 3:13–14 NIV).

The mirror that James urges us to look into in order to do self-evaluation is the Word of God. Looking into the Word of God is like taking that first grisly, gruesome, shocking look at yourself in the mirror early in the morning. Wow! The image in the mirror is who you really are, before washing your face, brushing your teeth, combing your hair, and putting on makeup! But here is the thing we have to be reminded of daily: when we see our flaws, imperfections, and shortcomings, we do everything within our power to change them through personal grooming. This should be the same action that we take when self-evaluating ourselves in the Word of God. James describes the person who doesn't try to change in this way: "Anyone who listens to the word but does not do what it says is like someone who looks at his face in a mirror and, after looking at himself, goes away and immediately forget what he looks like" (James 1:23–24 NIV).

What happens when we lean over to take a closer look at ourselves in the Word of God? First, the Word makes us free. The Word gives us freedom not just when we look into it, but also when we continue in it. I was driving through a small town named Dry Pong in central Louisiana and saw a very interesting saying posted on a church sign. The sign said, "The Bible is most powerful when we open it." Opening our Bibles, reading them, and applying the Word to ours lives is able to loosen whatever chains have us bound.

Where there is freedom, the blessings of God will soon follow. The promise is that we will be blessed in what we do. Earlier in this book, James tells us that the person who endures temptation is blessed. Now he wants us to know that the person who hears and does the Word of God is also blessed.

Self-Sacrifice

What makes our religion real? What makes our religion more than knowledge or a feeling, impulse, or emotion? Self-sacrifice is a component that makes our religion real. What does this self-sacrifice involve? It involves putting the needs of others before our own. Jesus puts it this way: "Love your neighbor as yourself" (Matthew 22:39 NIV), and "Do to others as you would have them do to you" (Luke 6:31 NIV).

Real religion requires us to guard our tongues. Just because you think or feel it does not mean you have to say it. Later on in this epistle, James reveals to us the destructive nature of the tongue. If we are not able to control our tongues as a bit is used to control a horse, then our religion is at best empty, worthless, and unprofitable. It serves no purpose. God does not desire empty, worthless, and unprofitable religion; He longs for religion that is pure and faultless. This type of religion manifests itself through caring and character.

"Religion that God our Father accepts as pure and faultless is this: to look after orphans and widows in their distress" (James 1:27 NIV). Caring for those who can't care for themselves is the type of religion that meets God's approval. We are to care for the helpless in such a way that they come to know the height, depth, width, and length of God's love. Real religion is all about ministering to the least of these. Jesus says, "Truly I tell you, whatever you did for one of the least of these brothers and sisters of mine, you did it for me" (Matthew 25:40 NIV). Real religion is at its best when we minister to the sick, hungry, imprisoned, and disenfranchised of society.

Good character and conduct also play a major role in our religion being pure and faultless. We must strive to be unspotted, unstained, and unblemished by the world. Instead of the world impacting and influencing us, we must have an effect on the world in which we live. Paul commands, "Do not conform to the pattern of this world, but be transformed by the renewing of your mind" (Romans 12:2 NIV).

When we engage in self-evaluation, self-control, and self-sacrifice, then we can be assured of victory over self-righteousness and self-centeredness. There is victory in our Lord and Savior Jesus Christ.

CHAPTER 5

No Big I's and Little U's
James 2:1–13

Favoritism can be divisive and destructive to any family. When we read and study the book of Genesis, we learn that one of the things that caused Jacob's family to be so dysfunctional was favoritism. Jacob was the recipient of his brother Esau's blessing because he was their mother Rebekah's favorite. It was because of the unhealthy spirit of favoritism for some fourteen years, Jacob was in a sort of exile from the home he loved so dearly.

Rebekah's spirit of favoring one child over another was passed down to Jacob, because even within his immediate family, this unhealthy spirit reared its ugly head. Jacob favored his son Joseph over his other children. The Bible says, "Now Israel loved Joseph more than any of his other sons, because he had been born to him in his old age; and he made an ornate robe for him" (Genesis 37:3 NIV). Favoritism caused Joseph's brothers to hate him. They hated Joseph so much that they couldn't even speak a kind word to their own brother. And the dreams that Joseph had about reigning over his brothers only made matters worse.

Favoritism will not only destroy our biological families, but also our spiritual families. James commands these believers, "My brothers and sisters, believers in our glorious Lord Jesus Christ must not show favoritism" (James 2:1 NIV). Favoritism goes against everything that we believe as Christians. As a matter of fact, favoritism is also contrary to the teachings and life of Jesus. Zebedee's wife, the mother of James and John, found that when she wanted Jesus to show partiality toward her two sons. Favoritism always involves a favor. She asks of Jesus, "Grant that one of these two sons of mine may sit at your right and the other at your left in your kingdom" (Matthew 20:21 NIV). Jesus denied her request, because favoritism and partiality are contrary to the nature and will of God.

The favoritism that James speaks against was not biological or spiritual but social. Favoritism was shown to the rich in the local church while the poor were discriminated against. James helps us to see how favoritism undermines real religion.

Faith and Favoritism Don't Mix

Faith has everything to do with believing and not seeing. Listen to the faith talk of Paul: "For we live by faith, not by sight" (2 Corinthians 5:7 NIV). Instead of living by faith, these believers that James addresses in this epistle were living by sight. They gave too much attention to the appearance of people and not enough attention to their hearts. When the rich showed up for worship wearing gold rings and fine clothes, they were given the best seats in the house. However, the same type of hospitality was not shown to poor people who wore filthy clothes. The poor people were forced to stand or sit on the floor.

My brothers and sisters, as people of faith, we should never judge a book by its cover. James equates judging someone by their appearance or by how much money they have as evil. "Have you not discriminated among yourselves and become judges with evil thought" (James 2:4 NIV)? Favoritism is an evil that divides churches and prevents them from growing. Don't fall into the trap of being the Christian—or should I say, the so-called Christian who only deals with certain types of people. Rich or poor, educated or uneducated, white or black, prince or pauper, God has commanded us to love everyone.

Favoritism Doesn't Make Sense

James is quite practical. He offers some practical truth that we should really consider the next time we are tempted to show favoritism. James says, "Has not God chosen those who are poor in the eyes of the world to be rich in faith and to inherit the kingdom he promised those who love him" (James 2:5 NIV). As I read these words of James, I could not help but to think of that factual story told by

Jesus about the rich man and Lazarus. The rich man had everything the world had to offer. Jesus describes his wealth in this way: "There was a rich man who was dressed in purple and fine linen and lived in luxury everyday" (Luke 16:19 NIV). But there was a problem; this rich man was bankrupt when it concerned his faith. Every day of his life, he focused on his riches, and not one moment was spent worshipping or thanking God for his blessings.

Lazarus's life was much different. Life hadn't been fair to Lazarus. Lazarus was poor, sick, homeless, and hungry. The Bible says, "At his gate was laid a beggar named Lazarus, covered with sores, and longing to eat what fell from the rich man's table. Even the dogs came and licked his sores" (Luke 16:20–21 NIV). But Lazarus was rich in faith. Life's trials, pain, and poverty have a way of strengthening the faith of the believer. Lazarus's faith in God allowed him to take hold of the promises of God when he died. Luke writes, "The time came when the beggar died and the angels carried him to Abraham's side" (Luke 16:22 NIV). Tragically, the rich man's lack of faith led to eternal damnation. Yes, the rich man died and went to hell, were he experienced unquenchable thirst, unending torment, and unimaginable pain.

These believers were foolish to show favoritism to the rich, because the rich didn't care about them at all. The rich were the cause of their mistreatment, exploitation, and legal problems. The rich had also disrespected their God. People consumed and controlled by riches speak evil against God easily. Paul commands us not to be like the rich who act this way. "Command those who are rich in this present world not to be arrogant nor to put their hope in wealth, which is uncertain, but to put their hope in God, who richly provides us with everything for our enjoyment" (1 Timothy 6:17 NIV). It just doesn't make sense to appease people who don't care about you or God.

Favoritism Is Sin

In order to show the fallacy of favoritism, James quotes directly from the Old Testament. "Love your neighbor as yourself" (Leviticus 19:18 NIV). When we discriminate against and dishonor the poor, we violate God's law. We disobey what James calls God's royal law when we show favoritism. Sin is sin. It doesn't matter what the sin is; if you break the law, you are a lawbreaker. The moral purity of God and His holiness, righteousness, and justice do not allow big and little sins. Just as God is displeased by sins such as adultery, murder, stealing, and coveting, He is not pleased with favoritism.

So we must make every effort to do away with favoritism. Do away with favoritism by not harming the poor. "Love does no harm to a neighbor" (Romans 13:10 NIV). Do away with favoritism by building up the poor. "We who are strong ought to bear with the failings of the weak and not to please ourselves. Each of us should please our neighbors for good, to build them up" (Romans 15:1–2 NIV). Do away with favoritism by speaking the truth to the poor. "Therefore each of you must put off falsehood and speak truthfully to your neighbor, for we are all members of one body" (Ephesians 4:25 NIV). Do away with favoritism by not judging the poor. "There is only one Lawgiver and Judge, the one who is able to save and destroy. But you-who are you to judge your neighbor" (James 4:12 NIV). We must do away with favoritism, because if we want God to be merciful unto us, then we must be merciful unto others, even the poor. Showing mercy makes our religion real.

CHAPTER 6

Authentic Christian Compassion
James 2:14–26

James 2:14–20 has been at the heart of controversy for centuries. This letter, addressed to the twelve tribes scattered abroad, written by James the brother of Jesus, almost didn't make it into Bible because of the controversy surrounding it. This letter was nearly excluded from the canon of scripture because it was believed that the teachings of James in verses 14–20 contradicted the teachings of Paul in his epistles to the church. In his letters, Paul argues clearly and passionately that we are saved by faith in Jesus Christ alone. Paul declares in Galatians, "Know that a person is not justified by the works of the law, but by faith in Jesus Christ. So we, too, have put our faith in Christ Jesus that we may be justified by faith in Christ and not by the works of the law, because by the works of the law no one will be justified" (Galatians 2:16 NIV). Yet in his very practical letter, James argues clearly and passionately that faith without works is dead.

47

Fortunately, the book of James is a part of the Bible today because when we do a close and thorough examination of the teachings of James and Paul, we discover that their writings are actually in agreement. The doctrines of Paul and James are in accord when we read Paul's words to the church at Ephesus. Paul writes, "For we are God's handiwork, created in Christ Jesus to do good works, which God prepared in advance for us to do" (Ephesians 2:10 NIV). Therefore, both Paul and James agree that we are saved by faith, but they also agree that we display our faith or prove that our religion is real through our works.

Faith and works go hand in hand when it concerns authentic Christian compassion. A consequence or result of genuine Christian faith is Christian compassion. How can you tell if a person's faith is the real thing? You can tell by how much compassion they show toward others. Real religion is seen at its best when we have authentic Christian compassion.

Authentic Christian Compassion Is More than Lip Service

According to the *American Heritage Dictionary*, "Lip service is a verbal expression or agreement unsupported by real conviction or action." James says, "What good is it, my brothers and sisters, if someone claims to have faith but has no deeds? Can such faith save them" (James 2:14 NIV). Can that type of faith save? That is a very valid question raised by James, because we all must be warned of the fact that there is no saving power in faith that is not genuine. James challenges believers to make sure their faith is genuine. We are to make sure our faith goes beyond lip service, because genuine faith is able to save, and it is most definitely beneficial. In this verse, James uses what is called the subjunctive mood in Greek. It is the mood of potentiality and possibility. When our faith is not backed up, confirmed, or solidified by authentic Christian compassion, there is a great possibility that our faith is not genuine. There is great potential for lip service.

What does lip service look like in the life of the Christian? We pray, teach, preach, and sing about compassion. However, when it is time to go out on the street and share the gospel of Jesus Christ, we are nowhere to be found. When it is time to visit the sick, our schedules are too full. We major in lip service, but we minor in ministry.

In a sense, we mimic and model the faith and actions of the conservatives and liberals of the 1990s. Bill Clinton said about the conservatives, "Compassionate conservatism was summed up by the following: 'I want to help you. I really do. But you know. I just can't.'" Then conservatives challenged Bill Clinton, because what he said did not line up with his lifestyle when the Monica Lewinski controversy came to light. This is the sort of thing that James addresses directly. "Suppose a brother or a sister is without clothes and daily food. If one of you says to them, 'Go in peace; keep warm and well fed,' but does nothing about their physical needs, what good is it?" (James 2:15–16 NIV) James wants us to move beyond empty words. My brothers and sisters, we can't just speak to problems and command them to go away. We have to stop just speaking to spiritual and social problems. But we have to move into action in order to do something about the problems that plague our world today.

Authentic Christian Compassion Is Produced by Living Faith

If faith without works is dead, then faith with works is living. Unfortunately, our faith becomes a dead corpse in the cemetery when there is no work to back it up. How can you distinguish between an organism that is dead and an organism that is alive? Living organisms produce. Have you ever looked at a living plant and artificial plant side by side? They look, feel, and even smell the same in most cases. However, one is living, and one is dead. One is able to produce, and the other is not. What type of faith do you have? Is it artificial or the real thing? Is it dead faith or living faith? A. W. Tozer, in his book *Experiencing God*, suggests that faith must be more than a definition to us; it must be action. There comes a time in life when faith must not just be a noun, but also manifest itself by being a verb. Jesus put it this way: "Make a tree good and its fruit will be good, or make a tree bad and its fruit will be bad, for a tree is recognized by its fruit" (Matthew 12:33 NIV).

The anonymous author of Hebrews gives to us many examples of saints that had living faith or faith put into action. Abel brought. Enoch was taken. Noah built. Abraham obeyed, believed, and sacrificed. Isaac blessed and worshipped. Moses refused, left, persevered, and kept. The challenge is offered to us by James, "Show me your faith without deeds, and I will show you my faith by my deeds" (James 2:18 NIV). Like Abraham, if we have living faith, then we can also be called the friends of God. Like Rahab the prostitute, our living faith will be honored and remembered by God.

Authentic Christian Compassion Distinguishes Us from Devils and Demons

James attempts to show these believers the importance of having genuine faith, real religion, and authentic Christian compassion by suggesting that faith without works is equivalent to the faith of devils and demons. James says to these Jewish Christians, "You believe that there is one God. Good! Even the demons believe that-and shudder" (James 2:19 NIV). James highlights the fact these Jewish Christians were monotheistic. "Hear, O Israel: The LORD our God, the LORD is one" (Deuteronomy 6:4 NIV). Every time the Jews went to worship, they quoted this verse, affirming their belief in the one, true, and living God. However, James literally cuts these believers by letting them know that devils and demons also believe that there is one God.

When we study the gospels, we learn that demons

have an intellectual awareness of who God is that is based upon terror and fear, not faith. Jesus encountered a demon-possessed man while teaching in the synagogue of Capernaum. In his gospel, Mark writes, "Just then a man in their synagogue who was possessed by an impure spirit cried out, 'What do you want with us, Jesus of Nazareth? Have you come to destroy us? I know who you are the Holy One of God'" (Mark 1:23–24 NIV). Jesus cast demons out of a crazy man in the tombs, and as they begged Jesus not to torment them, they acknowledged who He was. "What do you want with me, Jesus, Son of the Most High God? In God's name don't torture me" (Mark 5:7 NIV).

The demons know who God is, but they do not love or serve Him. The faith of demons and devils is void and empty. As followers of Christ, we must have the faith of disciples, not demons. As we follow Jesus, we must mimic and model His authentic Christian compassion.

In Mark 1:41, Jesus is moved with compassion and touches the leper, cleansing him of his leprosy. In Luke 7, Jesus has compassion and raises the widow's son from the dead. In Matthew 15, Jesus has compassion when He sees the hunger of the people, so He feeds the multitude, and in Matthew 20, Jesus has compassion on the two blind men sitting beside the road. The ultimate display of the Master's compassion was when He went to the cross, died for our sins, and rose three days later so our religion can be real.

CHAPTER 7

The Pink Tornado
James 3:1–12

One of the biggest and greatest lies ever told by a person is, "Sticks and stones may break my bones, but words will never hurt me." It is a bold-faced lie, because words most definitely hurt. And to suggest that words do not cause hurt and harm is contrary to the teachings of the Bible. The most devastating and destructive sins among the body of Christ are not the sins committed with the hands or feet. Sexual immorality and lust do not produce the most catastrophic results. The greatest devastation is caused by the pink tornado. The sins produced by the tongue are the worst. What we say to and about one another causes the most damage in the body of Christ.

James wants us to understand that just as tornados uproot trees, destroy homes, and take innocent lives, evil and hurtful words can be just as harmful. The pink tornado has caused churches to split, church members to stop speaking to or deal, with one another, and people to

53

walk away from the church, never to return. Marriages, friendships, and relationships have been wrecked because of the tongue. Therefore, we must learn to control our tongues. Think before you speak! Watch what you say! Be careful not to offend others with offensive or obscene words!

I believe that James 3 is the key to understanding the rest of the book. It serves as the glue that keeps this book together. James is trying to show us that real religion and controlling the tongue go hand in hand. In every chapter of this book, James speaks of some sticking, scandalous, sickening sins of the tongue.

James warns us in James 1:6 NIV, "But when you ask, you must believe and not doubt, because the one who doubts is like a wave of the sea, blown and tossed by the wind." Asking God for anything in the midst of unbelief and wavering is a sin. He then goes on to let us know later on in chapter 1 that saying God is the cause of sin and temptation is in itself a sin. "When tempted, no one should say, 'God is tempting me.' For God cannot be tempted by evil, nor does he tempt anyone" (James 1:13 NIV). Stop lying about God! We also sin with our tongues when we talk too much and never shut up. Yes, when we don't think before we speak or let anger control our tongues. "My dear brothers and sisters, take note of this: Everyone should be quick to listen, slow to speak and slow to become angry" (James 1:19 NIV).

In the first paragraph of James 2, the sin of the tongue

is the sin of blasphemy. James raises the question, "Are they not the ones who are blaspheming the noble name of him to whom you belong?" (James 1:7 NIV) Next, James commands us to speak as those who are going to be judged by God's law. We should not allow our tongues to be enslaved by the low, depraved standards of this world. "Speak and act as those who are going to be judged by the law that gives freedom" (James 1:12 NIV). Throughout the rest of chapter 2, James highlights and spotlights the reality that just saying we have faith is sinful, because it is equivalent to the faith of demons and devils.

Even in James 4, we are warned about the sins of the tongue. "When you ask, you do not receive, because you ask with wrong motives, that you may spend what you get on your pleasures" (James 4:3 NIV). It is sinful to ask for things that are contrary to the Word of God. It is also sinful to boast, according to James. "As it is, you boast in your arrogant schemes. All such boasting is evil" (James 4:16 NIV). James commands us in chapter 5 not to sin with our tongues by murmuring against one another and judging one another. Finally, James commands us not to swear. "Above all, my brothers and sisters do not swear not by heaven or by earth or by anything else. All you need to say is a simple 'Yes' or 'No'" (James 1:12 NIV).

Yes, the pink tornado is very destructive. It is stronger than a F6 tornado when unchecked. Therefore, James in chapter 3 helps us to see why the tongue needs to be controlled.

The Tongue Is Small but Powerful

The average size of the human tongue is ten centimeters long. The tongue seems to be very insignificant, but in reality, it is very powerful. Recognizing clearly the power of the tongue, James warns those of us who are responsible for teaching the Word of God. Those who have been called to teach God's Word are held to a higher standard by God; therefore, we will be held to a higher condemnation. James says, "Not many of you should become teachers, my fellow believers, because you know that we who teach will be judged more strictly" (James 3:1 NIV). Preaching and teaching the Word of God is nothing to play with. God will hold us accountable for every word we speak about His inspired, inerrant, and infallible Word.

The same God who will judge teachers will also judge those within the body of Christ who are not teachers. Therefore, none of us have right to look down on someone else because of sin. James reminds us, "We all stumble in many ways" (James 3:2 NIV). We all have some vices that have tripped us up along the way. You may not be guilty of fornication, adultery, murder, idolatry, blasphemy, or stealing, but we all have sinned with our tongues. Mean, hateful, harmful, and hurtful bullets have been shot from our mouths, and we will never be able to take them back.

James alludes to the fact that if we can control our tongues, then it is a sign that we can control the rest of our bodies. James is a great illustrator. He illustrates this point by comparing the tongue to a bit in the horse's mouth and a rudder that steers a very large ship. A teeny, tiny bit is able to control a humongous horse. Wow! By using the bit, you can make the horse go left and right, stop, and go. When our tongues are under the divine influence of the Holy Spirit, He who controls our tongue will also be in complete control of our other instruments. Big ships ride the mighty waves of the sea and are also able to withstand storms. It is the small rudder that helps the big ship navigate the sea and stay on course. In life, we too are going to travel through storms, and sometimes it is extremely hard to stay on course. However, if we can keep our tongues from attacking, blaming, and cursing God and others, then it will be easy for us to stay on course. Job was able to stay on course, because he controlled his tongue. Controlling his tongue was the key to his integrity. Job 1:22 NIV says, "In all this, Job did not sin by charging God with wrongdoing." Then Job 2:10 NIV declares, "In all this, Job did not sin in what he said."

In Proverbs, Solomon gives to us some heavenly wisdom as it concerns our tongues. An uncontrolled tongue brings strife. "The lips of fools bring them strife, and their mouths invite a beating" (Proverbs 18:6 NIV). An uncontrolled tongue is a snare. "The mouths of fools are their undoing, and their lips are a snare to their very lives" (Proverbs 18:7 NIV).

The Tongue Is Like a Fire

One of the most dangerous aspects of a fire is that if it is not controlled or put out, it will spread. Within Christendom, I believe that there are some fires that we want to spread. But then there are others that we want to contain. It is a beautiful thing to see a believer who is on fire for the Lord. The religion of those people is real, because their faith in Jesus Christ is the real thing. They are excited about worship, working, and witnessing for Jesus. They have great zeal for God! This is the type of fire that we want to spread among believers. However, the fire that is produced by an uncontrolled tongue is one that needs to be contained because of its destructive nature and power.

Solomon was correct when he wrote, "The tongue has the power of life and death, and those who love it will eat its fruit." What we say can bring life or death! What we say can build someone up or tear him or her down! What we say can lead someone to Christ or drive him or her away! Here, James shows us the tongue's ability to destroy and take life, just like a wildfire does in the forest. All it takes is a small spark to set a forest on fire. Then the next thing you know, people have lost precious property and loved ones. A lifetime of work and memories are turned into ashes.

Poison flowing from our tongues seems to have the same type of deadly effect. An uncontrolled tongue leads one down a similar, deadly, destructive, dooming course, just as temptation does in James 1. It is this deadly, destructive, dooming destination that eventually leads to the destruction of the soul in hell. James warns, "The tongue also is a fire, a world of evil among the parts of the body. It corrupts the whole body, sets the whole course of one's life on fire, and is itself on fire by hell" (James 3:6 NIV). It is a chain reaction of destruction, because an evil tongue leads to an evil body. An evil body leads to an evil world, which ultimately leads one to that evil place called hell. Oh, my brothers and sisters, please be very careful about what you say, because if you can't control your tongue, there is a very good chance that your religion is not real.

The Greek word for *hell* used in James 3:6 is the word *gehenna.* In the Old Testament, this word represented a place called the Valley of Hinnom, where a perpetual fire burned. The fire burned continually, because this was the place where the Jews burned their trash. It was a very stinky, filthy, and nasty place. It saddens me to say that we have more stinky, filthy, and nasty trash come from our mouths than there was in this trash dump just outside of Jerusalem. God will hold us accountable for the ungodly and unrighteous words that come from our mouths.

The Tongue Is Untamed

James is in agreement with Moses concerning the biblical truth that humankind has been able to tame every animal that is a part of God's creation. God the Creator has given humanity dominion over all animals. This is made crystal clear from the doctrine of creation found in Genesis 1. Moses says, "Then God said, 'Let us make mankind in our image, in our likeness, so that they may rule over the fish in the sea and the birds in the sky, over the livestock and all the wild animals, and over all the creatures that move along the ground" (Genesis 1:26 NIV). Anyone who would attempt to argue against humankind's dominion over animals, birds, reptiles, and sea creatures should take a trip to the zoo. Or even better, visit the Aquarium of America, and don't forget to view the mighty creatures of the sea that have been tamed.

People have tamed animals, birds, reptiles, and sea creatures. But we can't tame our tongues, which is a serious problem. James says, "But no human being can tame the tongue. It is a restless evil, full of deadly poison" (James 3:8 NIV). It is obvious that our tongues have not been tamed because of the contradictory words that proceed from our mouths. One minute, we are praising God. Then with the same mouth in the next minute, we are cursing everyone out. We celebrate God and then turn around and condemn those made in His image and likeness. God is not pleased with this sort of behavior. Fresh water and salt water do not come out of the same spring. Fig trees don't produce olives, and olive trees don't produce figs. There is a serious danger in being double-tongued.

We may not be strong enough to tame our tongues, but with God, all things are possible. God has made His mighty, matchless, and magnificent power available for us to tame whatever is ruining our lives. The power that is available to us is the same power that God used to raise Jesus from the dead. The resurrection of Christ is proof that God can tame our tongues. It is proof that the pink tornado is no match for the true and living God.

CHAPTER 8

Just Do It
James 3:13–18

When one hears or sees the three famous words, "Just do it," the first thing that probably comes to mind is Nike. For years, "Just do it" has been the advertising slogan for one of the most powerful and popular shoe companies in the world. Wherever one sees the Nike swoosh, "Just do it!" comes to mind. On the football gridiron, it doesn't matter if you are playing offense, defense, or special teams—just do it! On the hardwood basketball court, we are inspired to just do it! On the baseball diamond, whether in the outfield or infield, just do it! Not matter what arena you find yourself in as you live life, just do it!

"Just do it" should also be the mindset of a person who has real religion. A true Christian has the mindset of Paul when he declares, "I can do all this through him who gives me strength" (Philippians 4:13 NIV). When Jesus is your power source, all things are possible. It is this type of mindset that helps one to endure even the harshest circumstances and situations.

This section of James 3 informs us that wisdom is a characteristic of real religion. Authentic and genuine religion manifests itself not in wisdom that is only talked about, but also in wisdom that is put into action. In so many words, James wants us to just do it. Listen to the question that James asks: "Who is wise and understanding among you?" (James 3:13 NIV) I believe it is safe to say that when this question was asked in the first-century synagogue, all the people probably raised their hands. They went up because, everyone wants to be wise. No one wants to be considered a fool. James enlightens us by revealing to us that true wisdom is not based upon what we say but what we show. It is not based upon how we talk about wisdom but how we walk out wisdom in our daily lives. It is not based upon our lip service but our lifestyles. James says, "Let them show it by their good life, by deeds done in humility that comes from wisdom" (James 3:13 NIV).

Wisdom is not based upon our knowledge of Hebrew and Greek. Wisdom is not predicated upon how well we can exegete a text. Wisdom has nothing to do with our hermeneutics or homiletics. Wisdom has nothing to do with how many doctrines we know or scriptures we can quote. Wisdom has nothing to do with the letters in front of or behind our names. Wisdom has nothing to do with whether you graduated *summa cum laude, magna cum laude,* or *cum laude.* True wisdom is about living a holy life.

Authentic wisdom is about knowing how to apply God's rich Word to our lives in a very practical and real way.

In order to be able to put our wisdom into action, we must know that all wisdom isn't good wisdom. James contrasts for us wisdom that comes from below and wisdom that comes from above. Worldly wisdom verses heavenly wisdom is the issue at hand.

Worldly Wisdom

How can we distinguish the wisdom of the world from wisdom that is from heaven? Wherever bitter envying and strife are present, worldly wisdom is at work. Bitter envy means the jealousy is piercing, sharp, pointed, and cutting. This is the case when we want something that belongs to someone else so badly that it eventually causes a severe fracture in the relationship. After all, it was the sin of envy that caused the fall of humankind in the Garden of Eden. Adam and Eve wanted what belonged to God. They were not content with the blessings of God, even though He had given them more than enough. God had given Adam authority (dominion over the animals), a job (keeping the garden), a wife (Eve), and all of the trees except for the tree of the knowledge of good and evil. So often, we are just like Adam. God has blessed us with much, but we still want to take what belongs to someone else.

When we contrast the actions of Adam with those of Solomon, we learn that you don't have to take or steal what

God will freely give if you ask. One of the reasons Adam and Eve desired the tree of the knowledge of good and evil was because they thought that it would make them wise. In 1 Kings 3, Solomon simply asked God for wisdom, and God gave it to him.

Selfish ambition or strife also is a characteristic of worldly wisdom. In the ancient Greek world, self-ambition was seen mainly in politics. Today, our nation is in bad shape because of all the unwise people holding political offices. We have too many people in politics who are busy promoting themselves and their own agendas instead of trying to help people. Whether you are Democrat or Republican, conservative or liberal, it takes working together, compromise, and unity to get things done. Partisan politics is not limited to Capitol Hill and the White House. The divisiveness that runs rampant in political arenas often creeps into the church. Envy and strife will fracture us personally and corporately. James says, "For where you have envy and selfish ambition, there you find disorder and every evil practice" (James 3:16 NIV). Our God is a God of order, and He does not tolerate confusion and evil among His people. Paul teaches, "For God is not the author of confusion and every evil work" (1 Corinthians 14:33 NIV).

Worldly wisdom is temporary and corruptible. It will not last. We can't make it in this world depending on philosophy, sociology, and psychology, but we can make it if we have Jesus. Worldly wisdom is unspiritual, because it focuses on me, myself, and I. It is simply selfish. It doesn't work, because if we are going to follow Jesus, then we must deny ourselves. Worldly wisdom is demonic, because it promotes satanic interest. Satan uses this type of wisdom to kill, steal, and destroy.

Heavenly Wisdom

When studying the Bible, we should always be thankful to God for spiritual conjunctions! The next paragraph of this section of James's writing begins with the word "but." James declares, "But the wisdom that comes from heaven ..." (James 3:17 NIV). He informs us that there is an alternative to the wisdom of the world. Our lives don't have to be controlled by the world's earthly, unspiritual, and demonic wisdom. Heavenly wisdom is one of those good and perfect gifts that God sends down from above. What is heavenly wisdom like?

Heavenly wisdom is pure. It is wisdom that is untainted and unstained by evil. This type of wisdom drives us to live holy and consecrated lives. Peter writes, "But just as he who called you is holy, so be holy in all you do; for it is written: 'Be holy, because I am holy'" (1 Peter 1:15–16 NIV). Real religion requires us to have pure hearts, minds, hands, and bodies. The Holy Spirit, who resides in us and presides over our lives, infuses and infects us with heavenly wisdom. What is inside us will eventually manifest itself on the outside. David's prayer to God was, "Create in me a pure heart, O God and renew a steadfast spirit within me" (Psalm 51:10 NIV).

Heavenly wisdom is considerate. It is the type of wisdom that places the needs of others first. We must always strive to be like Jesus, who was always kind and considerate to others. Being considerate is the direct opposite of the selfish and sensual person who has embraced the wisdom of the world. Jesus teaches, "So in everything, do to others what you would have them do to you, for this sums up the Law and the Prophets" (Matthew 7:12 NIV).

Heavenly wisdom is peace-loving. Wherever there is heavenly wisdom, there will be peace. It is in direct contrast to the conflict and confusion that arise with the wisdom of the world. Within the body of Christ and especially in the local congregation, we must sow seeds of peace and not confusion. Heavenly wisdom knows that God is peace. "And the peace of God, which transcends all understanding, will guard your hearts and your minds in Christ Jesus" (Philippians 4:7 NIV).

Heavenly wisdom is submissive. Wisdom from above is evident when we submit to the authority of God. It is not only evident when we submit to the authority of God, but also when we also submit to whatever other authority God has blessed us with. Authority is a blessing, because God covers us with those whom He places in authority over us. Pastors are a covering for the local church. Husbands are covering for their wives. Parents are a covering for their children. Coaches are covering for players. Teachers are covering for students. The author of the book of Hebrews says to us, "Have confidence in your leaders and submit to authority, because they keep watch over you as those must given an account. Do this so that their work will be joy, not a burden, for that would be of no benefit to you" (Hebrews 13:17 NIV).

Heavenly wisdom is full of mercy and good fruit. Yes, the good fruit of compassion will be displayed in the life of the person who receives wisdom from above. There is a blessing in being merciful. The mercy that we show to others will be reciprocated to us. "Blessed are the merciful, for they will be shown mercy" (Matthew 5:7 NIV).

Heavenly wisdom is impartial and sincere. This type of wisdom doesn't engage in favoritism, and it is real. It doesn't look down on the poor or look up to the rich. Jesus is the center of joy for the person who has heavenly wisdom.

So just do it! Put your wisdom into action! Sow seeds of peace, and reap a great harvest of righteousness. Ask God to give you this wisdom from above. Seek heavenly wisdom so you can be used by God in a great way!

CHAPTER 9

When God Is Defriended
James 4:1–10

The word *defriend* has become very popular in today's culture, mainly because of social media. The Urban Dictionary defines *defriend* in this way: "To remove someone from your Livejournal, MySpace, Facebook, or other social networking site. Doing this is often seen as a passive-aggressive move, telling the person without telling them that you no longer want to be friends. It's also commonly a response to drama. Defriending often causes more drama." Have you ever wondered why there is so much drama in your life? Why is there so much conflict and confusion in the world? Why are there so many problems in the church? The answer to these questions can be found in the sad and terrible reality that we have defriended God to be friends with the world.

The Bible is crystal-clear about the fact that God wants to be our friend. It is God's desire to regain the relationship and fellowship He had with people before the fall in the

Garden of Eden. However, too often, we try to substitute true and genuine friendship with God by doing some very ungodly things. We grasp unsuccessfully for what only God can give. We try to cover up what can only be cleansed by the blood of Jesus. The friendship and fellowship with God that was lost in Eden because of Adam's sin was regained because of Jesus's sacrifice on the cross. This is a fact highlighted in Paul's teaching on justification: "For just as through disobedience of the one man the many were made sinners, so also through the obedience of the one man the many will be made righteous" (Romans 5:19 NIV).

The righteousness of God was credited to Abraham because of Abraham's faith; therefore, James calls Abraham God's friend. James teaches us, "Abraham believed God, and it was credited to him as righteousness and he was called God's friend" (James 2:23 NIV). Faith in Christ opens the door for genuine and real friendship with God. Hallelujah! We are no longer the enemies of God, but we are now the friends of God. Hallelujah! God's divine grace has caused a change in the relationship. Hallelujah! When Lebron James left the Cleveland Cavaliers in order to go the Miami Heat, he was the most hated man in Ohio. Lebron James was considered to be the enemy. However, when Lebron James went back to the Cleveland Cavaliers, the relationship changed. He is no longer hated; he is loved. He is no longer an enemy; he is a friend.

In the gospel of John, Jesus gave to His disciples the greatest honor by calling them His friends. Jesus says, "I no longer call you servants, because a servant does not know his master's business. Instead, I have called you friends, for everything that I learned from my father I have made known to you" (John 15:15 NIV). Please understand, saints of God, that the disciples' friendship with the Lord was born out of His love for them, based upon their obedience to His commands, and ultimately led to them bearing fruit in Him. A life of fruitlessness is the mark of one who is not God's friend.

James opens James 4 by asking these believers about all the problems that were going on in the world in which they lived. James asks, "What causes fights and quarrels among you?" The cause was their friendship with the world. They were fighting and quarreling with one another because instead of being friends with God, they were friends with the world. They coveted what others had, so they killed to get what they wanted. They devalued the sanctity of life for the purpose of material gain. Their religion was not real. Therefore, James points to the fact that we can't be friends with the world and with God at the same time. It just doesn't work that way!

When We Defriend God, Our Prayer Life Suffers

Prayer is one of the greatest privileges of the Christian. Prayer is the key to the kingdom. Prayer is the believer's key to access God's mercy in our times of need. The writer of Hebrews says, "Let us then approach God's throne of grace with confidence, so that we may receive mercy and find grace to help us in our time of need" (Hebrews 4:16 NIV). One of the most powerful moments of my life was when I heard my mother's doctor pray these words of scripture just before each of her two breast cancer surgeries. This doctor knew that in our times of greatest need, we must consult and seek out the Chief Physician, Jesus Christ. I believe that in his letter to the church at Ephesus, Paul encourages Christians not to live as spiritual paupers, because we are rich in Christ by the privilege of prayer that we have in Christ. It is a privilege that those outside of Christ don't possess. Paul writes in Ephesians 3:12 (NIV), "In him and through faith in him we may approach God with freedom and confidence." There is no need to be afraid or bashful when approaching our heavenly Father.

As we approach God's throne confidently, Jesus assures us we can ask, seek, and knock. However, there are times when we ask, but there is no answer; we seek but don't find anything; and we knock, but the door never opens. The problem is not with God but with us. It is a sign that our prayer life is in trouble.

James reveals to us that our prayer life is suffering when our requests don't line up with God's Word. "When you ask, you do not receive, because you ask with wrong motives, that you may spend what you get on your pleasures" (James 4:3 NIV). Sometimes the average Christian's prayer requests looks like a child's Christmas list. All we want are things that will allow us to have fun and make life easy. Putting it simply, our motives are all messed up. We ask for the wrong reasons. We ask for stuff not to do good things, but to engage in evil and ungodly activities. We desire things to expand our own kingdoms instead of asking, seeking, and knocking to advance the kingdom of God. We ask for things to promote our own selfish agendas and not the plans of God. We seek our own glory and not the glory of God.

Have you ever considered why the prayer life of Jesus was so powerful? Why did God the Father continually answer and open doors for Jesus? It was because at the end of the day, no matter what Jesus asked for, His desire was always to be in the will of the Father. Jesus's unchanging, unwavering desire was to glorify the Father's name.

If our prayer lives are going to be fixed, then our prayers can't be driven by pleasure but by the Holy Spirit. A good and healthy friendship requires open lines of communication. God can't communicate with us, and we can't communicate with God when the world is standing between us. Don't let anything or anybody stand between you and God.

When We Defriend God, We Cheat on Him

It is made very clear from the very beginning of this letter that God frowns upon division. God frowns upon a divided mind. "But when you ask, you must believe and not doubt, because the one who doubts is like a wave of the sea, blown and tossed by the wind. That person should not expect to receive anything from the Lord. Such a person is double minded and unstable in all they do" (James 1:6–8 NIV). God also frowns upon a divided church. "My brother and sisters, believers in our glorious Lord Jesus Christ must not show favoritism" (James 2:1 NIV). In James 3, we discover that God frowns upon a divided tongue. "Out of the same mouth come praise and cursing. My brother and sisters, this should not be" (James 3:10 NIV). We learn in James 4:4 that the same God who frowns upon a divided mind, church, and tongue also frowns upon a divided heart. James says, "You adulterous people, don't you know that friendship with the world means enmity against God? Therefore, anyone who chooses to be a friend of the world becomes the enemy of God" (James 4:4 NIV).

James uses some very strong language to describe those whose hearts are divided between God and the world. They are identified as adulterers and enemies of God. These believers are accused of stepping out on God. They are guilty of cheating on God. There is tension; therefore, the relationship is not friendly but hostile. Real religion cannot and will not live in hostility with God. Only religion that is insincere and impure would try to play both sides of the fence. So a choice has to be made. Hate the world, and love God, or love the world, and hate God. Choose a healthy and whole friendship with God or an unhealthy and broken relationship with the world.

It really comes down to who will rule and reign over our lives. Who is going to call the shots in our lives? Just as God frowns upon divided minds, churches, tongues, and hearts, He also frowns upon divided loyalty. I leave you with the words of Jesus concerning this matter: "No one can serve two masters. Either you will hate the one and love the other, or you will be devoted to the one and despise the other. You cannot serve both God and money" (Matthew 6:24 NIV).

When We Defriend God, There Is a Way to Be Friends Again

When we defriend God, grace is available to repair the broken friendship. Every day, my brothers and sisters, we should continually thank God for His grace. Every day, God gives us a new day with new mercy. The grace of God reminds us that forgiveness is available when we go astray. Forgiveness is available when we choose the friendship of the world over the friendship of God. But this grace is only available and applicable to our lives when we humble ourselves before the Lord. James says, "But he gives us more grace. That is why scripture says, 'God opposes the proud but shows favor to the humble'" (James 4:6 NIV). God stands against the proud. God opposes those who think that they are better than others. God resists those who think and feel as if they don't need Him. But God smiles upon the humble. God's perpetual presence is among those who are meek and lowly in heart. "For those who exalt themselves will be humbled, and those who humble themselves will be exalted" (Matthew 23:12 NIV).

How does this humility that James speaks of flesh itself out in our lives? James gives a list of practical steps to get your friendship with God back on track: submit yourself to God, resist the Devil, draw near to God, purify your hearts, and humble yourself before the Lord.

Simply put, it is all about getting closer to God. It is about understanding that Jesus is the most genuine and greatest friend we can ever have.

CHAPTER 10

When You Know Better, You Do Better
James 4:11–17

One of the greatest fallacies among Christians down through the ages has been an attempt to place the sins of humanity into various categories. For centuries, the Catholic church has tried to classify sins into the categories of venial sins and mortal sins. Venial sins are those sins that are considered to be excusable, minor, not so trifling, or not seriously wrong. However, mortal sins are more severe, grievous, or deadly than other sins.

Classifying sins as venial or mortal goes totally against what the Bible teaches. John, the old apostle and beloved disciple of Jesus, declares, "All wrongdoing is sin, and there is sin that does lead to death" (1 John 4:17 NIV). John was not saying that some sin is more severe than other sin but trying to emphasize and reveal how the mercy of God operates in our lives. John wants us to understand that when God gets fed up with us, death can come with any sin. James puts it this way: "Then, after desire has conceived, it gives birth to sin; and sin, when it is full-grown, gives birth to death" (James 1:15 NIV).

It is a very dangerous thing to classify sins, because when we engage in such activity, it causes us to tolerate, become numb, or even overlook certain sins within the body of Christ. James offers a word of warning to us as he highlights some of these sins. "If anyone, then, knows the good they ought to do and doesn't do it, it is sin for them" (James 1:17 NIV).

James Warns Us Not to Judge Others

The first command that James gives is very clear. We are not to speak evil against one another. Christians have no business slandering another person's name. Nor should we murmur and complain about those whom God has placed in authority in the body of Christ. We should do our very best to avoid the children of Israel syndrome. All throughout their wandering in the wilderness, they murmured and complained about their leader, Moses. However, the main focus of James is this passage of scripture is about believers judging one another. Condemning others has no place in the life of a Christian.

James says, "When you judge the law, you are not keeping it, but sitting in judgment on it" (James 4:11 NIV). We can't referee the game and play at the same time. One of the biggest messes ever when I was growing up was playing in a basketball game where the players called their own fouls. When I called foul, traveling, double dribble, or hand checking on someone else, it was always the right call. However, when the tables were turned and someone called a violation on me, it was always the wrong call. Sadly, my friends had the same attitude. It led to fighting, fussing, and factions on the basketball court. I believe it is safe to say that judging others also leads to fighting, fussing, and factions in the church.

Who do we think we are to judge someone else? When we judge others, it is obvious that we think we are above the law and do not have to play by the rules of the game. For us to think that we are above the law is to think that we are God. And none of us is qualified to be God, because He is unique in holiness, unmatched in righteousness, and unyielding and upright in justice.

James Warns Us Not to Jump to Conclusions about Tomorrow

It is not of God to jump to conclusion and assume things about tomorrow. In order to illustrate his point, James pulls an example from businessmen of the first century who made plans to travel, buy, sell, and make a whole lot of money in the process. Now, we must be careful not to take what James is trying to teach out of its proper context. There is nothing wrong with planning. As a matter of fact, in order to be successful in any endeavor, there must be some short-term and long-term planning. You have probably heard it said before, "If you fail to plan, then plan to fail." I often heard my childhood pastor say, "Prior preparation prevents poor performance."

We mess up when we omit God from our future plans. And if He is not omitted from our plans, then He sure is not a priority in our planning. When planning a wedding, we make plans for flowers, food, dresses, tuxedos, banquet halls, and even wine. Then as an afterthought, we say, "We better get some counseling from the preacher to see what God says about marriage." God must always be part of our plans, because we do not know what tomorrow holds—but He does. We should never assume that tomorrow will come, because life is like a vapor; we can be here today and gone tomorrow. We must learn how to be like the saints of old who always made God a part of their plans. The saints of old would say concerning the future, "If it is the Lord's will."

However, accepting the will of God for our lives is often easier said than done. The will of God can often be filled with pain, suffering, and hardship. Jesus faces this painful reality in the Garden of Gethsemane because of what was ahead of Him. It is in the Garden Gethsemane—the place of pressing, crushing, and extraction—that Jesus confronts the fact that in just a little while, the total weight of human depravity, wickedness, and sinfulness would be on His shoulders. Christ knew that God the Father was able to deliver Him from the bitter cup of the crucifixion; however, He also knew that being delivered from the crucifixion was not the will of the Father. We too must be willing to trust

God's omnipotent power and divine will and purpose. Just as Jesus, we must submit to the will of the Father. "Yet not as I will, but as you will" (Matthew 26:39 NIV).

James Warns Us Not to Rejoice by Patting Ourselves on the Back

James warns us not to get caught up in the hype of people. We should not let people pump us up concerning our accomplishments, or we will begin to praise ourselves. This type of boasting is described by James as evil, hurtful, satanic in nature, sick, and degenerate. "As it is, you boast in your arrogant schemes. All such boasting is evil" (James 2:16 NIV). James concludes this chapter by putting forth a challenge to the Christian who has real religion. "If anyone, then, knows the good they ought to do and doesn't do it, is sin for them" (James 4:17 NIV). It is a challenge for us to do what we know is right, is holy, and brings glory to God and not to ourselves.

What is the right thing to do when it concerns the boasting and bragging of the believer? Instead of boasting about our own accomplishments, we should boast about what Jesus accomplished on the cross. Boast about God's redemptive work through His Son, Jesus Christ. The apostle Paul was a man who could have boasted and bragged about a number of his personal accomplishments. Paul could have boasted about being circumcised on the eighth day of the people of Israel. He could have patted himself on the back for being from the tribe of Benjamin, a Hebrew of

Hebrews, and a Pharisee. Paul did not boast in any of these things but chose to boast about the cross of Jesus Christ.

Paul boasts in his letter to the churches of Galatia, "May I never boast except in the cross of our Lord Jesus Christ, through which the world has been crucified to me, and I to the world" (Galatians 6:14 NIV). I have been married to my wife Tiffany now for twelve years, and this is the scripture that I had written on the groom's cake for our wedding. Even on my wedding day, one of the most important days of my life, I wanted to boast about the cross of Jesus Christ. Every Christian who has real religion should be willing to boast about the sacrificial and vicarious death of the Lord Jesus Christ. Whatever we do, we must do it for the glory of God.

CHAPTER 11

Real Faith

James 5

Most biblical scholars and theologians suggest that if you want to see a beautiful portrait of faith, then you should take a look at Hebrews 11. It is in Hebrews 11 that we find the definition of faith and many examples of what faith looks like. The author of Hebrews defines faith in this way: "Now faith is confidence in what we hope for and assurance about what we do not see" (Hebrews 11:1 NIV). Faith for the Christian is standing on present and future realities in Christ that we cannot see with the physical eye. The examples of faith given by the writer of Hebrews show us that faith has to be more than a definition for Christians; it has to be put into action. James also makes this same point in James 2 when he teaches us that the fruits of genuine, real faith are works. As James closes this letter to Jewish Christians scattered throughout the world, he paints his own portrait of what real faith looks like.

Real Faith Does Not Trust in Riches

James begins by warning the rich who hadn't listened to the words of Jesus. "Do not store up for yourselves treasures on earth, where moth and vermin destroy, and where thieves break in and steal. But store up for yourselves treasures in heaven, where moths and vermin do not destroy, and where thieves do not break in and steal. For where your treasure is, there your heart will be also" (Matthew 6:19–21 NIV). The rich are destined for misery, because they chase after earthly riches and not the true, everlasting riches of heaven. They would soon understand the temporary nature of their earthly riches. All of their money, clothes, gold, and silver would soon waste away. My brothers and sisters, just as gangrene attacks and eats away at the human body, the wealth of those who put their trust in riches will be consumed in the same way. Loving riches more than God will not only infect and impact our material possessions, but if we are not careful, it will also gnaw away at our souls.

Trusting in riches also causes many people to become cruel. The wealthy in the text preferred to hoard their wealth instead of paying fair wages to those who had worked hard in their field. When I read this passage, I am reminded of the fight and struggle going on today throughout America to raise the minimum wage. There are those who claim to be religious who fight fiercely against raising the minimum wage because they argue that low wages have nothing to do with morality. They make this argument because they believe that wages are set by an amoral market. However, James argues that wages have everything to do with morality and faith. He says to the rich who are guilty of oppressing the poor, "Look! The wages you failed to pay the workers who mowed your fields are crying out against you. The cries of the harvesters have reached the ears of the Lord Almighty" (James 5:4 NIV).

When the cries of the oppressed penetrate the ears of God, there will always be a response. It is good to know that our cries do not fall upon deaf ears! David testifies to this comforting assurance: "I waited patiently for the LORD: he turned to me and heard my cry" (Psalm 40:1 NIV). Too often, our cries for help are ignored by people and the world. However, it is good to know that God is always listening. God always sees, hears, and acknowledges real faith.

Knowing that God hears and sees our struggle gives the oppressed the hope of roles one day being reversed with those of the oppressors. Right now, the oppressors are on top, and the oppressed are on the bottom. The innocent seem to be losing while the guilty seem to be winning. But James speaks of a time when the roles will be reversed. "You have lived on earth in luxury and self-indulgence. You have fattened yourselves in the day of slaughter. You have condemned and murdered the innocent one, who was not opposing you" (James 5:5–6 NIV). The tide will most definitely change when the end comes. It will be similar to the role reversal seen in Luke 16 with the rich man and

Lazarus. Real faith is guaranteed to be rewarded in the life to come. Paul puts it this way: "For physical training is of some value, but godliness has value for all things, holding promise for both the present life and the life to come" (1 Timothy 4:8 NIV).

Real Faith Awaits the Return of Christ

Faith in Jesus Christ gives us hope for the future and help for today. It is a faith that is rooted and grounded in Jesus's teaching about the end times and eschatology. It is an irrefutable fact that Jesus is coming back one day. The return of Christ is inevitable, indefinite, and imminent. Christ's return is inevitable, because whether we like it or not, He is coming back, and there is nothing we can do to stop Him. Christ's return is indefinite, because no one knows the day or hour of His return. Christ's return is imminent, because He is coming quickly. And until the Lord returns, we are to be patient. James says, "Be patient, then, brothers and sisters, until the Lord's coming" (James 5:7a NIV).

What does James mean when he commands these Christians to be patient? Sometimes in life, we find ourselves in situations where patience is needed. If you have ever had to wait in a long line at the airport or wait on a flight that has been delayed, then you know a little something about being patient. Or maybe you have endured a long wait at the doctor's office; then you also know what patience is all about. However, patience in this text is more about being patient in the midst of pressure and persecution. Many Greek scholars define this sort of patience as passion under control. When trials and tribulations creep unexpectedly into our lives, patience is all about self-discipline. Patience is all about doing good and doing what is right, even when things are not going so well in our lives. That is the type of patience that James commands from these Christians.

James is practical in this letter to first-century saints when he gives examples of how we are to be patient as we await the return of Christ. First, we are to be patient as a farmer. "See how the farmer waits for the land to yield its valuable crop, patiently waiting for the autumn and spring rains. You too, be patient and stand firm, because the Lord's coming is near" (James 5:7b–8 NIV).

The farmer labors tirelessly, day after day, only to wait patiently for the harvest. The time in which he sows is totally under his control; however, the time of reaping is totally in the hands of the almighty God. We systematically sow by planting and watering, working and toiling, only to wait for God to supernaturally bless what we have sown into the soil. It is during this season of waiting that we must refrain from grumbling against one another and judging one another.

The second example that is given to us is that of the prophets. They teach us how to be patient in the midst of suffering. Great men of God such as Elijah, Elisha, and Jeremiah did what was good and right even when facing evil. When those from Jeremiah's home town of Anathoth plotted evil schemes against him, he waited on God. How did Jeremiah wait on God? Jeremiah committed his cause to God. Jeremiah sent his problems and persecutors into exile. He banished them from his life when he placed them in the hands of God. It is a little easier to be patient in the midst of suffering and affliction when you know God's got your back.

The final example is Job. Oh, what a great example of waiting on God! Job did not have a good day. Job did not have a bad day. Job had a downright ugly day. Job woke up one morning the greatest, richest, most respected man in the East, but by the time he went to bed, his life had been turned upside down. Job lost his family, fortune, and fame, but he didn't lose his faith. The Bible says, "In all this, Job did not sin by charging God with wrongdoing" (Job 1:22 NIV).

What does James mean when he talks about Job enduring and persevering? It is the picture of someone not running away or quitting when things get tough. Job reminds us that when we don't run away or quit when times get tough; that is when God will give us double for our trouble. God also has a way of turning our situations around. Job 41:10 (NIV) says, "After Job had prayed for his friends the LORD restored his fortunes and gave him twice as much as he had before." What an awesome God we serve!

As we await the return of Christ, we must be patient.

As we await the Lord's return, our *yes* must be *yes*, and our *no* must be *no*. James shows us that there is no need to swear by heaven or earth when your faith is real.

Real Faith Engages in Prayer

James begins this section of his letter with a series of questions and answers. If you are in trouble, then the answer is prayer. If you are happy, then the answer is singing praises to God. If you are sick, then pray and go to the doctor. If you have sinned, then confess your sins and pray. Over and over again, the answer to this litany of questions is prayer. And the answer to the litany of problems in life is also prayer. Whether the problem is physical, spiritual, or emotional, the answer is prayer. We must literally send our desires, wants, and needs toward God, who is able to do above and beyond what we can even imagine.

James makes the argument that a righteous life unleashes the power of God in our lives. "The prayer of a righteous person is powerful and effective" (James 5:16b NIV). Sin limits the power of God in our lives. It is as if we place a leash on God that prevents Him from doing the great things He wants to do for us when our lives are out of line with His will. We also limit the power God in our lives when we make the mistake of trusting in our own righteousness and not the righteousness of God. Therefore, James urges us to follow the example of the prophet Elijah. The key to Elijah's successful and powerful prayer life was the fact that he prayed earnestly. Nothing could prevent or distract him from talking to God. Nothing hindered Elijah from asking God for what he needed and wanted. Elijah's earnest prayer life stopped and started the rain. (See 1 Kings 17:1, 18:42.)

Real Faith Goes after Sinners

James concludes this practical letter to the believers of the first century by placing emphasis on evangelism. However, the evangelistic emphasis is not just outreach, but also includes in-reach. Real faith and religion care about those who wander away from the truth. What should our response be when a brother or sister walks away from the church? James answers that question for us when he says, "Someone should bring that person back" (James 5:19b NIV). Those who walk away from the church do not likely turn around intransitively; it happens transitively. In other words, they do not usually turn themselves around; someone has to go after them in order for them to come back to the Lord.

We must intentionally and aggressively go after backsliders and sinners, because walking away from God can and will lead to physical death. Going after them saves a soul from death and covers a multitude of sins—yes, all different colors and shades of sin. Hallelujah! The same God who saves lives also forgives sin. God releases us from sin, restores back to us what we lost because of sin, and gives us rest from the guilt and shame of sin. God pulled back the cover by revealing Himself to the world through Jesus so our sins could be covered by His precious blood. God the Father sent Jesus into the world after us, and now He is sending us out into the world to go after sinners who are seeking religion that is real.

Made in the USA
Las Vegas, NV
12 March 2022